Antarctica

Antarctica presents an overview of the geography of this continent. The teaching and learning in this unit are based on the five themes of geography developed by the Association of American Geographers together with the National Council for Geographic Education.

The five themes of geography are described on pages 2 and 3. The themes are also identified on all student worksheets throughout the unit.

Antarctica is divided into seven sections.

Each section includes:
* teacher resource pages explaining the activities in the section
* information pages for teachers and students
* reproducible resources
    maps
    note takers
    activity pages

Pages 4–6 provide suggestions on how to use this unit, including instructions for creating a geography center.

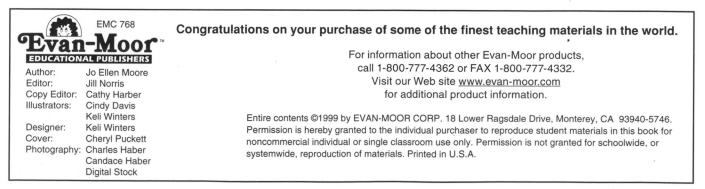

EMC 768

Evan-Moor™
EDUCATIONAL PUBLISHERS

Author: Jo Ellen Moore
Editor: Jill Norris
Copy Editor: Cathy Harber
Illustrators: Cindy Davis
              Keli Winters
Designer: Keli Winters
Cover: Cheryl Puckett
Photography: Charles Haber
              Candace Haber
              Digital Stock

Congratulations on your purchase of some of the finest teaching materials in the world.

For information about other Evan-Moor products,
call 1-800-777-4362 or FAX 1-800-777-4332.
Visit our Web site www.evan-moor.com
for additional product information.

Entire contents ©1999 by EVAN-MOOR CORP. 18 Lower Ragsdale Drive, Monterey, CA 93940-5746. Permission is hereby granted to the individual purchaser to reproduce student materials in this book for noncommercial individual or single classroom use only. Permission is not granted for schoolwide, or systemwide, reproduction of materials. Printed in U.S.A.

The Five Themes of Geography

·Location

Position on the Earth's Surface

Location can be described in two ways. **Relative location** refers to the location of a place in relation to another place. **Absolute location** (exact location) is usually expressed in degrees of longitude and latitude.

McMurdo Research Station is located south of Mt. Erebus near Ross Sea.

Amundsen Sea is located at 70°S latitude, 110°W longitude.

·Place

Physical and Human Characteristics

Place is expressed in the characteristics that distinguish a location. It can be described in **physical characteristics** such as water and landforms, climate, etc., or in **human characteristics** such as languages spoken, religion, government, etc.

Antarctica receives so little precipitation, the continent is a desert.

There are nopermanent settlements, but many countries maintain research stations in Antarctica.

·Relationships within Places

Humans and the Environment

This theme includes studies of how people depend on the environment, how people adapt to and change the environment, and the impact of technology on the environment. Cities, roads, planted fields, and terraced hillsides are all examples of man's mark on a place. A place's mark on man is reflected in the kind of homes built, the clothing worn, the work done, and the foods eaten.

Because of the extreme weather conditions in Antarctica, many stations place water and sewage lines above ground for easier maintenance.

Movement

Human Interactions on the Earth

Movement describes and analyzes the changing patterns caused by human interactions on the Earth's surface. Everything moves. People migrate, goods are transported, and ideas are exchanged. Modern technology connects people worldwide through advanced forms of communication.

> Radios, satellites, and computers are used by scientists at Antarctic research stations to communicate with the rest of the world.

Regions

How They Form and Change

Regions are a way to describe and compare places. A region is defined by its common characteristics and/or features. It might be a geographic region, an economic region, or a cultural region.

> Geographic region: The Antarctic Peninsula is one region of Antarctica.
> Economic region: There is no private business or industry in Antarctica.
> Cultural region: There are research stations from many countries, each maintaining the culture of its own country.

Using This Geography Unit

Good Teaching with *Antarctica*

Use your everyday good teaching practices as you present material in this unit.

- Provide necessary background and assess student readiness:
  - review necessary skills such as using latitude, longitude, and map scales
  - model new activities
  - preview available resources
- Define the task on the worksheet or the research project:
  - explain expectations for the completed task
  - discuss evaluation of the project
- Guide student research:
  - provide adequate time for work
  - provide appropriate resources
- Share completed projects and new learnings:
  - correct misconceptions and misinformation
  - discuss and analyze information

Doing Student Worksheets

Before assigning student worksheets, decide how to manage the resources that you have available. Consider the following scenarios for doing a page that requires almanac or atlas research:

- You have one classroom almanac or atlas.

  Make an overhead transparency of the page needed and work as a class to complete the activity, or reproduce the appropriate almanac page for individual students. (Be sure to check copyright notations before reproducing pages.)
- You have several almanacs or atlases.

  Students work in small groups with one resource per group, or rotate students through a center to complete the work.
- You have a class set of almanacs or atlases.

  Students work independently with their own resources.

Checking Student Work

A partial answer key is provided on pages 77 and 78.

Consider the following options for checking the pages:

- Collect the pages and check them yourself. Then have students make corrections.
- Have students work in pairs to check and correct information.
- Discuss and correct the pages as a class.

Creating a Geography Center

Students will use the center to locate information and to display their work.

Preparation

1. Post the unit map of Antarctica on an accessible bulletin board.
2. Add a chart for listing facts about Antarctica as they are learned.
3. Allow space for students to display newspaper and magazine articles on the continent, as well as samples of their completed projects.
4. Provide the following research resources:
   * world map
   * globe
   * atlas (one or more)
   * current almanac
   * computer programs and other electronic resources
   * fiction and nonfiction books (See bibliography on pages 79 and 80.)
5. Provide copies of the search cards (pages 69–71), crossword puzzle (pages 72 and 73), and word search (page 74). Place these items in the center, along with paper and pencils.

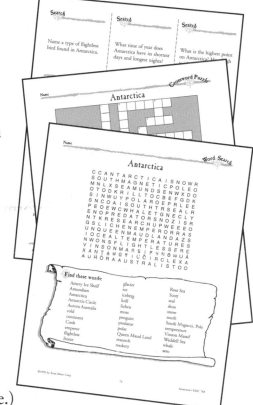

Additional Resources

At appropriate times during the unit, you will want to provide student access to these additional research resources:

* Filmstrips, videos, and laser discs
* Bookmarked sites on the World Wide Web (For suggestions, go to http://www.evan-moor.com and click on the Product Updates link on the home page.)

Making a Portfolio on Antarctica

Provide a folder in which students save the work completed in this unit.
Reproduce the following portfolio pages for each student:

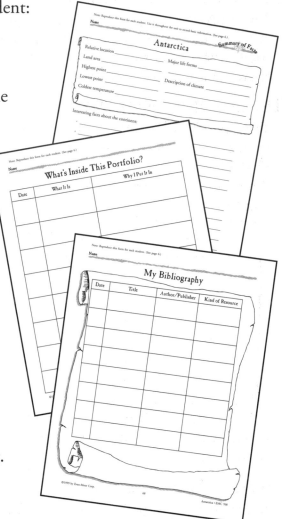

- A Summary of Facts about Antarctica, page 66
  Students will use this fact sheet to summarize basic
  information they have learned about Antarctica.
  They will add to the sheet as they move through the
  unit.

- What's Inside This Portfolio?, page 67
  Students will record pages and projects that they
  add to the portfolio, the date of each addition,
  and why it was included.

- My Bibliography, page 68
  Students will record the books and other materials
  they use throughout their study of Antarctica.

At the end of the unit have students create a cover
illustration showing some aspect of Antarctica.

Encourage students to refer to their portfolios often.
Meet with them individually to discuss their learning.
Use the completed portfolio as an assessment tool.

Using the Unit Map

Remove the full-color unit map from the center of this book and use it to help students
do the following:

- locate and learn the names of landforms, water forms, and physical regions of Antarctica
- practice finding relative locations using the cardinal directions shown on the
  compass rose
- calculate distances between places using the scale

Introducing Antarctica

Tour the Geography Center

Introduce the Geography Center to your class. Show the research materials and explain their uses. Ask students to locate the sections of atlases and almanacs containing material about Antarctica.

Thinking about Antarctica

Prepare a KWL chart in advance. Reproduce page 8 for each student. Give students a set period of time (5–10 minutes) to list facts they already know about Antarctica and questions about the continent they would like answered.

Penguins

Know	Want to Know	Learned

Transfer their responses to the KWL chart. Post the chart in a place where you can add to it throughout your study of the continent.

Where Is Antarctica?

Reproduce pages 9–11 for each student.

"Locating Antarctica" helps students locate Antarctica using relative location. Use the introductory paragraph to review the definition of relative location, and then have students complete the page.

"A Bird's-Eye View of Antarctica" shows students the two ways the continent is most commonly shown. Have students locate Antarctica on the unit map and on a globe and describe how the representations are different. Discuss which is a more accurate view and why.

"Name the Hemisphere" reviews the Earth's division into hemispheres. Students are asked to name the hemispheres in which Antarctica is located. Using a globe to demonstrate the divisions, read the introduction together. Then have students complete the page.

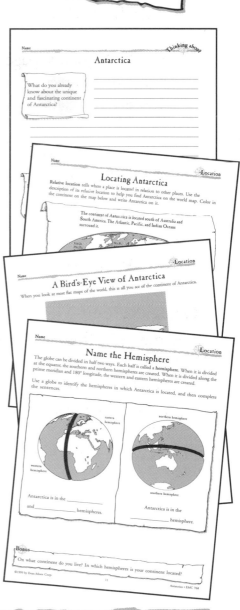

Name

Antarctica

What do you already know about the unique and fascinating continent of Antarctica?

_____
_____
_____
_____
_____

_____
_____
_____

If you could talk to someone who has been to Antarctica, what would you ask?

_____
_____
_____
_____
_____

_____
_____
_____

Locating Antarctica

Relative location tells where a place is located in relation to other places. Use the description of its relative location to help you find Antarctica on the world map. Color in the continent on the map below and write Antarctica on it.

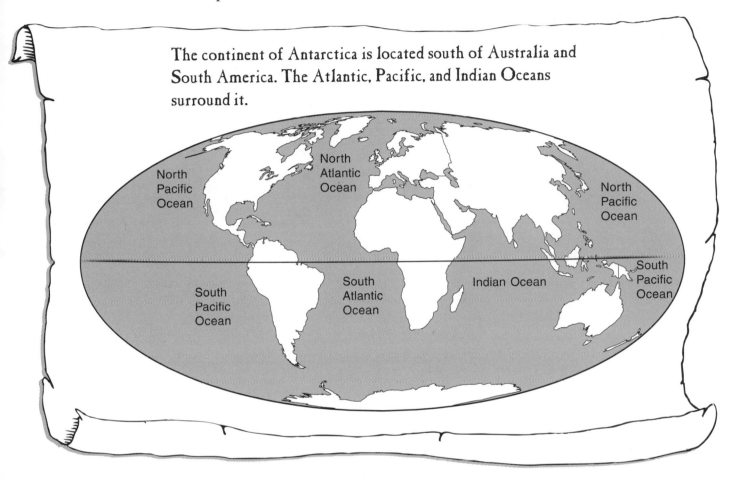

The continent of Antarctica is located south of Australia and South America. The Atlantic, Pacific, and Indian Oceans surround it.

North Pacific Ocean

North Atlantic Ocean

North Pacific Ocean

South Pacific Ocean

South Atlantic Ocean

Indian Ocean

South Pacific Ocean

Look at a map of Antarctica. Find these places and write their relative locations:

1. Ross Ice Shelf _____

_____

2. Antarctic Peninsula _____

_____

Bonus

Now write the relative location of Antarctica in relation to the country in which you live.

A Bird's-Eye View of Antarctica

When you look at most flat maps of the world, this is all you see of the continent of Antarctica.

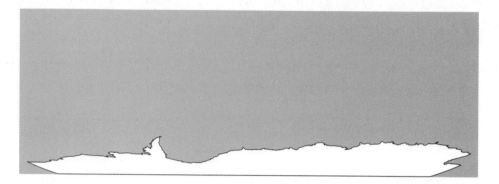

If you were a bird flying over the continent, this is what you would see.

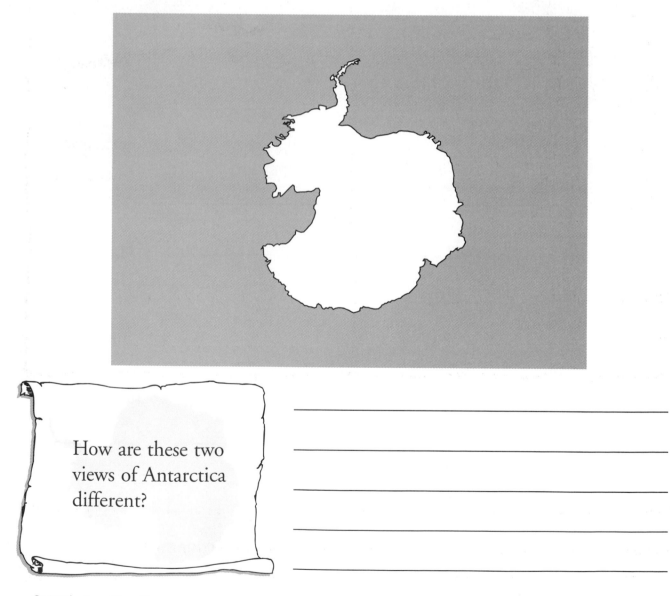

How are these two views of Antarctica different?

_____

_____

_____

_____

_____

Name the Hemisphere

The globe can be divided in half two ways. Each half is called a **hemisphere**. When it is divided at the equator, the southern and northern hemispheres are created. When it is divided along the prime meridian and 180° longitude, the western and eastern hemispheres are created.

Use a globe to identify the hemispheres in which Antarctica is located, and then complete the sentences.

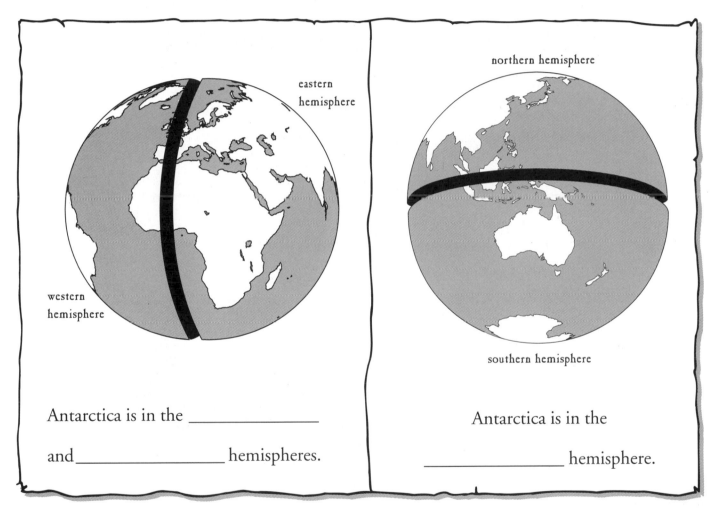

Antarctica is in the _____

and _____ hemispheres.

Antarctica is in the

_____ hemisphere.

Bonus

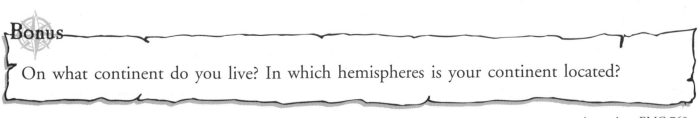

On what continent do you live? In which hemispheres is your continent located?

Water and Landforms

Collecting information by reading physical maps involves many skills. Pages 13–18 provide students with the opportunity to refine these skills as they learn about water and landforms on the continent of Antarctica.

Water Forms

Reproduce pages 13 and 14 for each student. Use the unit map to practice locating oceans and seas on a map.

- Discuss pitfalls students may face in finding the correct names (names written sideways and in small type, several names close together).
- Have students locate at least one example of an ocean and a sea on the unit map.
- Then have students locate and label the listed water forms on their individual physical maps.

Iceberg

Landforms

Reproduce page 15 for each student. Have students use the same map used to complete page 14, or reproduce new copies of page 13 for this activity.

- Review the ways mountains, ice shelves, and other landforms are shown on a map (symbols, color variations, labels).
- Have students practice locating some of the landforms on the unit map of Antarctica.
- Then have students locate and label the listed landforms on their individual physical maps.

A Cross Section of Antarctica

Reproduce page 16 for each student. Explain that the illustration shows what a section of Antarctica might look like if it were cut down the middle. Discuss the different kinds of information shown on the cross section and then answer the questions together.

Longitude and Latitude

Reproduce pages 17 and 18 for each student. Use a map to review how to use lines of longitude and latitude to determine exact locations. Then have students complete the activity independently.

Antarctica

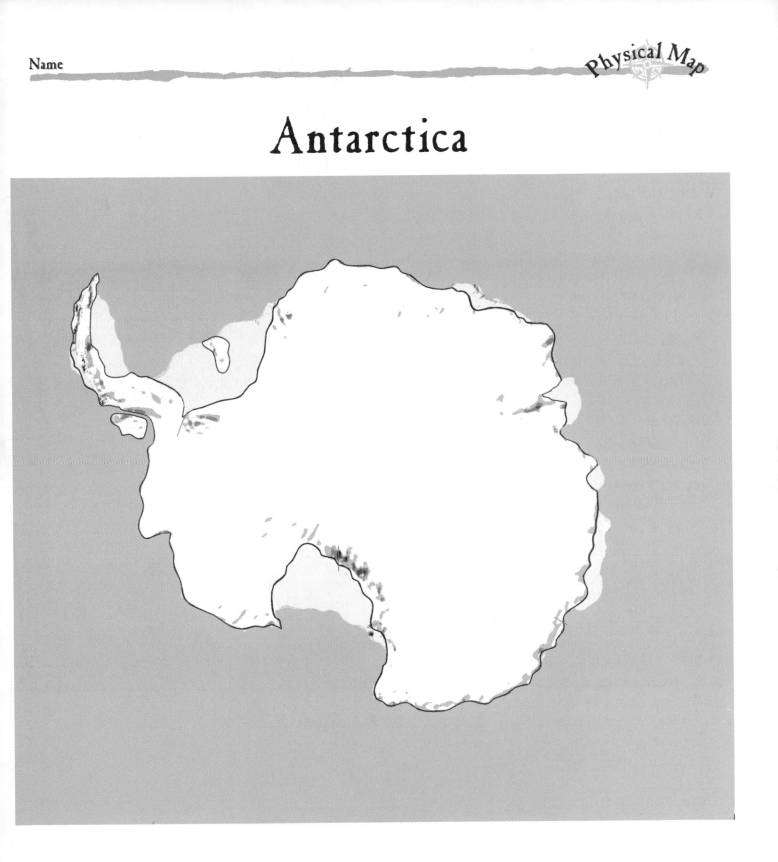

Water Forms of Antarctica

Find these places on your map of Antarctica and label them. Use a map, a globe, or an atlas to help you find the answers. Check off each one as you label it.

☐ Atlantic Ocean

☐ Indian Ocean

☐ Pacific Ocean

☐ Weddell Sea

☐ Ross Sea

☐ Bellingshausen Sea

☐ McMurdo Sound

☐ Amundsen Sea

☐ Bransfield Strait

☐ Prydz Bay

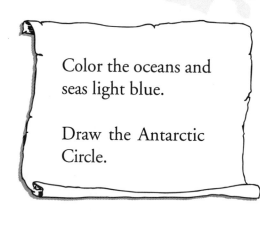

Color the oceans and seas light blue.

Draw the Antarctic Circle.

Bonus

Name the ocean that is nearest to where you live.

Landforms of Antarctica

Find these places on your map of Antarctica and label them. Use a map, a globe, or an atlas to help you find the answers. Check off each one as you label it.

☐ Antarctic Peninsula

☐ Queen Maud Land

☐ Wilkes Land

☐ Marie Byrd Land

☐ Enderby Land

☐ Coats Land

☐ Ross Ice Shelf

☐ American Highland

☐ Ronne Ice Shelf

☐ Filchner Ice Shelf

☐ Amery Ice Shelf

☐ Transantarctic Mountains

☐ Mount Erebus

☐ Vinson Massif

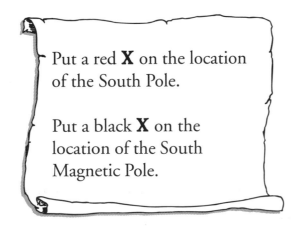

Put a red **X** on the location of the South Pole.

Put a black **X** on the location of the South Magnetic Pole.

Antarctica Cross Section

Use the information on this cross section of Antarctica to answer the following questions.

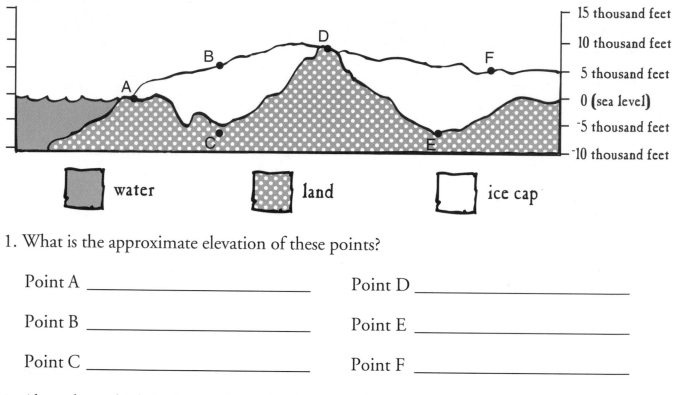

1. What is the approximate elevation of these points?

   Point A _____   Point D _____

   Point B _____   Point E _____

   Point C _____   Point F _____

2. About how thick is the ice from the bottom of the ice pack at point E to the top of the ice pack at point F?

   _____

Antarctica

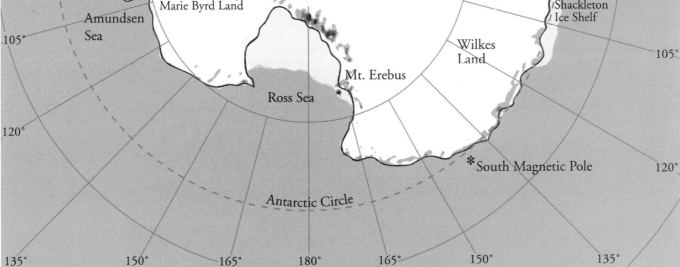

Longitude and Latitude

Lines of longitude and latitude are used to find exact (absolute) locations of places. Use the lines of longitude and latitude on your map to find what is located at these points.

Latitude	Longitude	Location
1. 75°S	180°	
2. 73°S	30°E	
3. 85°S	90°E	
4. 70°S	45°W	
5. 79°S	86°W	
6. 70°S	120°E	
7. 70°S	110°W	
8. 65°S	105°E	
9. 82°S	40°W	
10. 70°S	70°E	

Bonus

Write the exact (absolute) location of your hometown using longitude and latitude.

Geographic Regions

Most continents have a wide variety of regions—hot deserts, tree-covered forests, and wide, grassy plains. At first sight Antarctica seems to have just one region—a cold, icy one! It is a very cold place, but even in this land of snow and ice there are differences. These activities will help students identify some of those differences.

Begin by sharing books and videos about Antarctica. Have students observe and describe the variations in appearance of the different areas (areas of solid ice, areas with exposed rock, rocky shores, high mountains, flat expanses). Then have students do the following activities to explore some regions more closely.

Ice, Ice, and More Ice

Make an overhead transparency of page 20 and also reproduce a copy for each student. Refer to the map as you discuss the various "icy" regions of Antarctica. Ask students to use class resources (e.g., the World Wide Web) to answer questions such as these:

>"How thick is the ice sheet of the Polar Plateau?"
>"What is the average temperature at the South Pole?"
>"What special precautions do people at Amundsen-Scott Research Station have to take?"
>"How are ice shelves formed?"

Glaciers and Icebergs

Reproduce pages 21 and 22 for each student. Ask students to share what they already know about glaciers and icebergs. Record their responses on chart paper or the chalkboard. Next, have students read the information and do the experiment on page 21. Finally, have them use the information they have gathered, plus other class resources, to answer the questions on page 22.

The Antarctic Peninsula

Reproduce pages 23 and 24 for each student. Select a student to locate the Antarctic Peninsula on the unit map. Have students describe how this area differs from the rest of the continent (sticks out from the continent, reaches farther north, is long and narrow, more coastline touches water, etc.). Share appropriate sections of books such as *Summer Ice: Life Along the Antarctic Peninsula.*

Read and discuss the information on page 23 together. Ask students to explain how the location and shape of the peninsula allow more plants and animals to live in this region (more coastline to meet ocean currents, the peninsula is farther north so it is warmer, etc.). Students then answer the questions on page 24.

Ice, Ice, and More Ice

Most of the Antarctic continent is buried under thousands of feet of ice and snow. The mountains are icy. The plains are icy. The coastline is icy. Much of the time high winds blow the snow around.

Polar Plateau

Much of the interior of the continent is buried under a thick layer of ice. This area is named the Polar Plateau. Extreme cold, harsh winds and an altitude of 9300 feet (2835 m) have made it a difficult area to explore. Amundsen-Scott Research Station is located at the South Pole on the Polar Plateau. Buildings at the research station are covered by a large aluminum geodesic dome. Special clothing is required for working outside the dome.

Ice Shelves

Glaciers move slowly from high inland areas down to the sea. These huge sheets of ice move out over the water, forming ice shelves. In some places the ice shelf is 1000 feet (about 300 m) thick. Huge pieces break off into the ocean, forming icebergs.

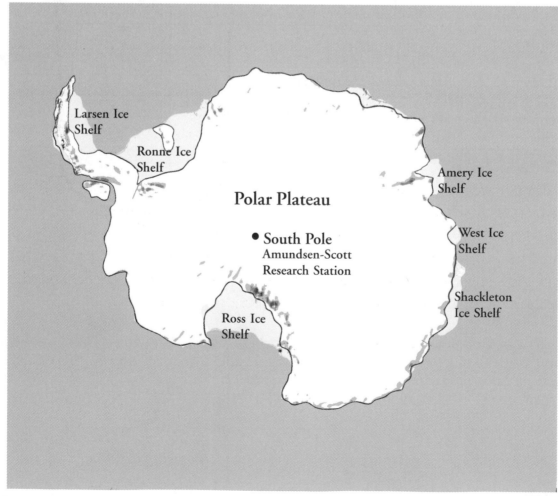

Name _____

Glaciers and Icebergs

Glaciers are formed from snow that fell hundreds of thousands of years ago. The mountains of snow became mountains of ice. The ice mountains are so large that they still haven't melted completely. Today the ice mountains on Antarctica move slowly as they melt. They flow like slow-moving rivers to the sea. These rivers of ice are called **glaciers.**

When the ice reaches the sea, it forms shelves of ice over the water. In some places the ice shelf is 1000 feet (300 m) thick. Sometimes huge pieces of the ice break off into the sea. These pieces of ice become **icebergs.**

Icebergs drift in the ocean for years before they finally melt. Even a small iceberg can take two or more years to melt.

Try this experiment to learn more about how icebergs behave.

Making an "Iceberg"

Materials

- water
- glass container
- ice cube

Steps to Follow

1. Fill your glass container with water.
2. Drop in the ice cube.
3. Observe your "iceberg."
4. Draw a picture of what you see.

When water freezes, it expands. This means the same volume of ice will always be lighter than the same volume of liquid water. This is why icebergs float. Follow the directions above to make your own miniature iceberg in a glass.

More about Glaciers and Icebergs

Use what you know and the resources in the geography center to answer these questions:

1. How are glaciers formed? _____

_____

2. How is it possible for a huge glacier to move? _____

_____

3. What is the difference between a glacier and an iceberg? _____

_____

4. How much of an iceberg is above the water and how much is below the surface?

_____

5. What makes icebergs turn into such unusual shapes? _____

_____

6. Why do icebergs often look white or blue instead of clear like ice cubes?

_____

Label this picture.

The Antarctic Peninsula

One place in Antarctica is "warm" in summer. At least, it is warmer than the rest of the continent. The west coast of the Antarctic Peninsula (also called Palmer Land or Graham Land) and the nearby islands extend north toward South America. Ocean currents and winds raise the temperature to a few degrees above freezing. The 24-hour summer sun melts some ice to provide meltwater. There is even some rainfall.

Exposed rock cliffs provide a place for lichens and mosses to grow. Two types of flowering plants grow at the northern tip of the peninsula.

Penguins and other birds come ashore on the peninsula and islands to mate and raise their chicks. Seals come ashore to molt. Whales travel along the peninsula searching for food.

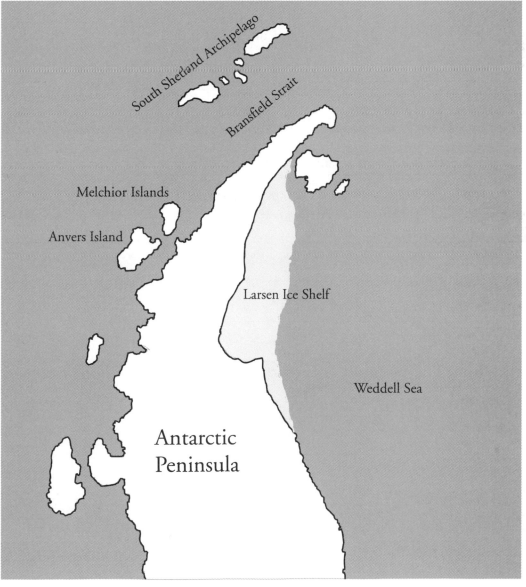

The Antarctic Peninsula

Use what you have learned about the Antarctic Peninsula and
information from class resources to answer these questions:

Penguin

1. Describe the land formation of the Antarctic Peninsula.

   _____

   _____

2. What is the approximate distance from the northernmost tip of the Antarctic Peninsula
   to the southernmost tip of South America?

   _____

3. Why is it warmer on the coast of the Antarctic Peninsula than the rest of the continent?

   _____

4. Name the three kinds of penguins that use the peninsula and nearby islands for rookeries.

   _____

5. Name the plants that grow on the Antarctic Peninsula. Explain where they get the
   water they need to grow.

   _____

   _____

   _____

   _____

Bonus

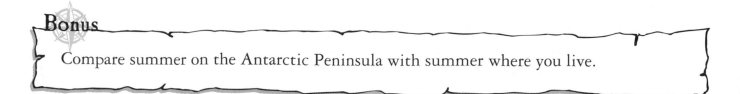

Compare summer on the Antarctic Peninsula with summer where you live.

Antarctic Plants and Animals

The harsh climate, lack of soil, and long periods of darkness make it difficult for plants or animals to live on the continent of Antarctica. Some small plants do manage to grow during the short summer growing season. Only tiny invertebrates live permanently on land. However, the oceans around Antarctica are teeming with plant and animal life.

Seal

Antarctic Plants

Reproduce pages 27 and 28 for each student. Share the information page with students, and then have them use class resources to find out more about the plants of Antarctica as they complete the activity page. (Books such as *Antarctica: The Last Unspoiled Continent* and *Our Endangered Planet—Antarctica* contain photographs of the few types of plants growing there.) Provide time for students to share what they discover.

Antarctic Animals

Introductory Activities

Begin by challenging students to name the Antarctic animals they know. List these on a chart and write a descriptive phrase after each name.

> penguin–a bird that cannot fly but can swim
> seal–a large mammal that swims in the sea
> killer whale–a small black-and-white whale that hunts for meat

Share books or show a video about Antarctic animals. Discuss the information learned from these sources, and add new animal names and descriptive phrases to the chart.

Animals in Antarctica

Reproduce page 29 for each student. Explain that animals throughout the world have adapted to the environment in which they live. Ask students to predict some of the ways that the seal and the penguin might have adapted to the harsh climate of Antarctica. Then have students use class resources to determine actual adaptations.

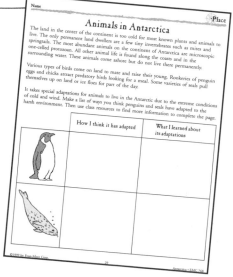

Antarctic Penguins

Reproduce pages 30 and 31 for each student. Divide the class into small groups. Each group will do the following:

- read and discuss the information page
- write an acrostic poem about penguins
- use class resources and World Wide Web resources to complete the penguin chart
- compare a bird living in their community to a penguin

Note: You will want to rotate groups through the center if your resources are limited.

Krill and the Food Web

Reproduce pages 32–34 for each student. Make an overhead transparency of page 33. Read and discuss the information page together, referring to the transparency to clarify the information. Have students complete the activity page independently.

Amazing Antarctic Animals

Reproduce pages 35 and 36 for each student. Send students to class resources to locate two interesting facts about each animal shown.

Antarctic Animal Report

Provide each student with a copy of the note taker on page 37. Have students choose one interesting Antarctic animal and use class resources to locate the information to complete the note taker. Then have students use the information to write a report about the animal.

Plants in Antarctica

Algae Covered Rocks

Even in the summer, most of Antarctica is covered in ice. However, during the short summer growing season some small plants do manage to grow in this harsh environment.

Plants tend to grow close to the ground or in the rocks for protection. Most algae grow on rocks where penguins have established colonies. Sheets of algae are strong enough to withstand the birds traveling back and forth to the sea. There are types of algae that grow on glaciers, sometimes making the ice cliffs look like they have been dusted with red or green powder.

A flat plant called lichen grows where rock is exposed to the surface. It grows most often on rocks with a northern exposure where the sunlight is most abundant. The rock cliffs become covered in shades of yellow, orange, and brown from the lichen. The plant is very slow growing. Footprints left in lichen will remain for years.

Mosses grow in thick clumps near bird colonies. Rich nutrients created by the birds' droppings feed the plants.

In parts of the Antarctic Peninsula, two flowering plants—a type of grass and a small pearlwort—grow on the small amount of sandy soil found there.

While few plants grow on the continent, the seas around Antarctica are full of plant life. Seaweed and algae even grow under the ice shelves.

Antarctic Plants

Algae

Lichen

Use your "Plants in Antarctica" information page and class resources to find the answers to these questions:

1. What kind of plant is...

    lichen? _____

    alga? _____

    moss? _____

2. Why do so few plants grow in Antarctica?

    _____

    _____

3. Explain why plants grow better in the oceans around Antarctica than on the land.

    _____

    _____

Bonus

Compare a plant that grows where you live with an Antarctic plant.

Animals in Antarctica

The land in the center of the continent is too cold for most known plants and animals to live. The only permanent land dwellers are a few tiny invertebrates such as mites and springtails. The most abundant animals on the continent of Antarctica are microscopic one-celled protozoan. All other animal life is found along the coasts and in the surrounding water. These animals come ashore but do not live there permanently.

Various types of birds come on land to mate and raise their young. Rookeries of penguin eggs and chicks attract predatory birds looking for a meal. Some varieties of seals pull themselves up on land or ice floes for part of the day.

It takes special adaptations for animals to live in the Antarctic due to the extreme conditions of cold and wind. Make a list of ways you think penguins and seals have adapted to the harsh environment. Then use class resources to find more information to complete the page.

	How I think it has adapted	What I learned about its adaptations

Penguins

Penguins are birds, but they are birds with these special differences:
- They have small feathers packed close together to keep them warm and dry.
- They rub oil over their feathers to make the feathers waterproof.
- They have webbed feet with claws. They use their feet like paddles when they swim. They dig into the ice with their claws.
- Their wings are shaped like paddles. They cannot fly, but they are great swimmers.
- Penguins waddle as they walk. They cannot run very fast, so they slide on their stomachs when they are in a hurry.
- Penguins must breathe air. When they are swimming, they leap out of the water to get air, then dive back in.
- Penguins are good parents. They never leave the nest unattended. The parents protect and feed their young until they can take care of themselves.
- Penguins dive into the sea for their food. They eat krill, fish, and squid.

Use the penguin facts above to finish the acrostic poem.

P _____

E _____

N _____

G _____

U _____

I _____

N _____

S _____

Antarctic Penguins

These penguins make their homes in Antarctica. Use class sources to find out more about them. Record the information you find on this chart.

	Emperor	Adélie	Gentoo	Chinstrap
Height				
Weight				
Markings				
Nesting habits				
Egg care				
Chick care				

Bonus

Compare and contrast a penguin with one kind of bird found where you live.

Krill and the Food Web

There are more nutrients in the Antarctic Ocean than in any other ocean. The violent winds and waves occurring in this area stir up the ocean's minerals and nutrient salts. The water is filled with tiny microscopic marine plants called plant plankton. Animal plankton eats plant plankton. Shrimplike animals called krill eat both kinds of plankton.

Krill travel in vast swarms throughout the Antarctic Ocean. These krill are the food for larger animals. In fact, almost all of the animals in Antarctica eat krill, or they eat something that has already eaten krill.

Krill is the oceans' largest single source of protein. It is also rich in vitamins. Some scientists think it may be a source of food for the hungry people of the world. Nutritionists are trying to find ways to improve the taste of frozen or dried krill.

Some countries, such as Japan, have already started krill fisheries. The processed krill is used as animal feed. It is also added to other meats, soups, etc., for people to use. Would you eat krill?

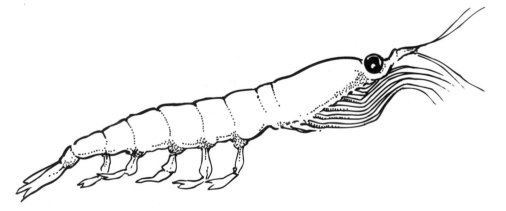

(This krill is shown about twice its actual size.)

Antarctic Food Web

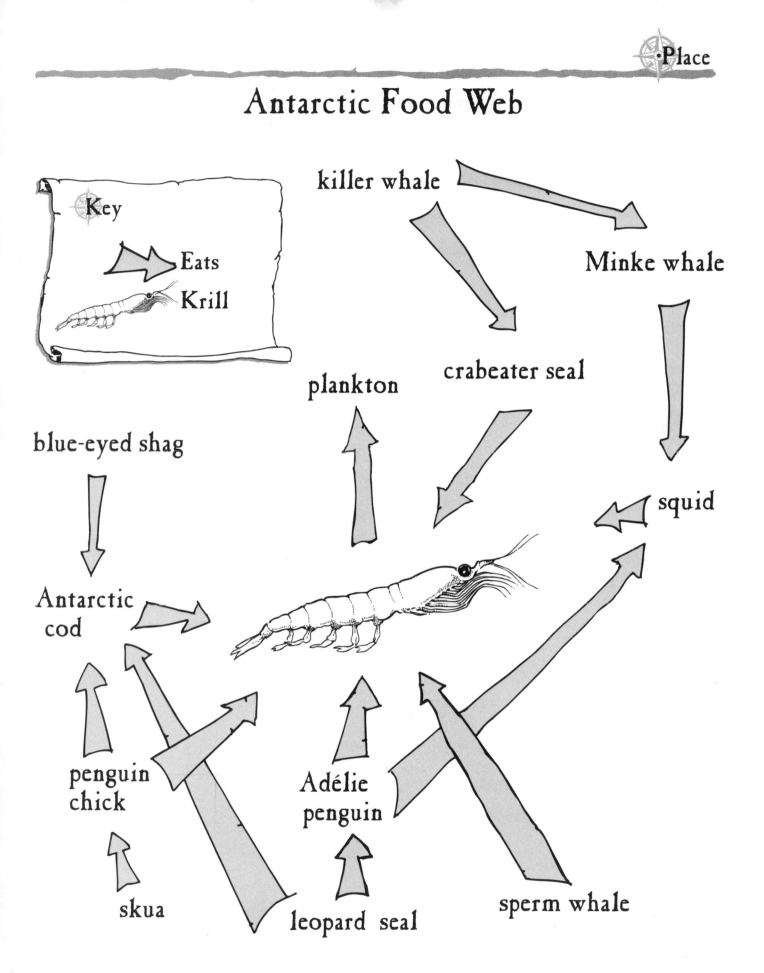

Key

Eats Krill

killer whale

Minke whale

plankton

crabeater seal

squid

blue-eyed shag

Antarctic cod

penguin chick

Adélie penguin

skua

leopard seal

sperm whale

Antarctic Food Web

Study the food web diagram to help you answer these questions:

1. Which animals eat krill?

_____

_____

2. What does a killer whale eat?

_____

_____

3. What does a krill eat?

_____

_____

4. What is the largest animal that eats krill?

_____

_____

5. Which animals eat squid?

_____

_____

Bonus

Think about where you might fit in a food web. Do you eat anything that comes from the sea? Where does it fit in an ocean food web?

Amazing Antarctic Animals

Name: Krill
Facts:

_____

_____

_____

_____

Name: Skua
Facts:

_____

_____

_____

_____

Name: Crabeater Seal
Facts:

_____

_____

_____

_____

Name: Leopard Seal
Facts:

_____

_____

_____

_____

Name: Weddell Seal
Facts:

_____

_____

_____

_____

Name: Albatross
Facts:

_____

_____

_____

_____

Antarctica • EMC 768

Place

Name: Orca
Facts:

_____

_____

_____

_____

Name: Gentoo Penguin
Facts:

_____

_____

_____

_____

Name: Emperor Penguin
Facts:

_____

_____

_____

_____

Name: Humpback Whale
Facts:

_____

_____

_____

_____

Name: Blue-eyed Shag
Facts:

_____

_____

_____

_____

Name: Antarctic Cod
Facts:

_____

_____

_____

_____

Animal Report Note Taker

Name of animal

Draw the animal here.

Physical characteristics:

- _____
- _____
- _____
- _____
- _____

Where does it live?	What does it eat? How does it get its food?
How does it protect itself?	Describe its life cycle.

The _____ is/is not endangered.

The Exploration

For centuries people were curious about what might be at the southernmost part of the Earth. Was there an unknown "southern land"? It wasn't until the 1820s that the first recorded sightings of the Antarctic continent occurred and its exploration began.

Most books on Antarctica have some information about the exploration of the continent. *The Cruelest Place on Earth: Stories from Antarctica; The Arctic and Antarctica, Roof and Floor of the World*; and *Antarctica* are a few of the books containing one or more chapters dedicated to exploration of the continent.

Exploring Antarctica

Reproduce pages 39–43 for each student. They are to cut the pages apart and staple them in order. As a class, read and discuss the information provided about each of these early explorers. Use other class resources, including the World Wide Web, to learn more about these brave men.

A Time Line of Exploration

Reproduce page 44 for each student. Have them use the Exploring Antarctica booklet and other sources to complete the time line. Students are to write the correct explorer's name with each date and event.

Encourage students to add additional dates, events, and explorers to the time line as they gain more knowledge.

A Race to the South Pole

Make an overhead transparency of pages 45 and 46 and also reproduce each page for each student. Share information about the two expeditions from class resources. Refer to the map as you review the routes taken by Scott and Amundsen. Fill in the fact chart together as students recall the two expeditions.

Exploring Antarctica

A little more than two hundred years ago, explorers began to travel farther and farther south in search of land. There was no recorded proof that land existed at the southern end of the world.

Early explorers met harsh conditions without the equipment and knowledge available to scientists today. Yet these brave men continued to push their way south on missions of discovery.

Here are some of those brave explorers.

1

Captain James Cook (U.K.)

In the 1770s Captain James Cook was sent by the British Admiralty to try to locate the southern continent to see if it really existed. Captain Cook and his crew became the first men known to have crossed the Antarctic Circle. They circumnavigated the continent without ever seeing it.

Cook managed to sail farther south than any other known explorer before harsh weather conditions made him abandon his search. Cook didn't know it, but he was only about 150 miles from the Antarctic coast.

2

Captain Fabian von Bellingshausen (Russia)

In 1819 Captain von Bellingshausen was sent by Czar Alexander I to explore the southern continent. He discovered Peter Island and Alexander Island while circling Antarctica. He sighted land, but thought it was just another ice field. He didn't realize until later that what he had seen was Antarctica.

Sealer Nathaniel Palmer (U.S.A.) and explorer Edward Bransfield (U.K.) both saw the Antarctic Peninsula shortly after Bellingshausen.

3

Charles Wilkes (U.S.A.)

Wilkes sailed from the United States to measure the Earth's magnetism and to establish a U.S. claim to at least part of Antarctica. In 1840 he sailed near the South Magnetic Pole, sighting a long coastline. He mapped a large stretch of the coast.

Wilkes was the first person to insist that what he had discovered was a continent.

4

Sir James Clark Ross (U.K.)

In 1841 Ross was the first explorer to penetrate the ice pack into Ross Sea. He discovered the Ross Ice Shelf and two volcanoes that he named after his ships, Erebus and Terror. He surveyed 500 miles of coastline.

Ross returned to Ross Sea in 1841, but his ship nearly sank when he collided with an iceberg during a storm. On this trip he surveyed parts of Graham Land (Palmer Peninsula).

5

Ernest Shackleton (U.K.)

Shackleton was part of an expedition with Captain Robert Scott in 1901. Illness and lack of food forced the expedition to turn back.

In 1907 Shackleton returned to Antarctica leading his own expedition, and came within miles (kilometers) of the South Pole before being forced by the harsh weather to turn back.

In 1914 Shackleton returned once again to Antarctica, planning to lead an expedition across the continent. The expedition ran into trouble when its ship became locked in the ice. The ice slowly crushed the ship. Shackleton and his men were stranded. They had to camp on the shifting ice floes for months. They were always cold and wet and lived on a diet of seal meat. Finally, the ice pack drifted north to open water, and they were able to launch their small boats and sail for land. In spite of continued difficulties faced by the expedition, not one man was lost during the two-year ordeal.

6

Roald Amundsen (Norway)

In 1900 Amundsen was made commander of the National Antarctic Expedition. He led several expeditions to Antarctica, making many scientific discoveries.

Amundsen's big dream was to be the first man to reach the South Pole. In 1911 he set out to make that dream come true. It took Amundsen and his party 56 days to reach his goal. On December 14 Amundsen became the first man to reach the South Pole. He arrived a few weeks ahead of an expedition commanded by Captain Robert Scott.

7

Captain Robert Falcon Scott (U.K.)

Captain Scott began planning his expedition in 1911, confident that he would succeed in his goal to be the first man to reach the South Pole. Shortly before his expedition left in 1911, Scott learned that Amundsen was also leading an expedition to the South Pole.

Scott planned to use motorized sledges, ponies, and dogs on the journey. This turned out to be disastrous. The motors failed and the ponies were not up to the harsh weather conditions. Progress was slow, and when Scott and his four companions reached the South Pole, they discovered that Amundsen had beaten them by a few weeks. The discouraged expedition turned back, but none of Scott's party survived the return trip. Their bodies and expedition notes were found months later.

8

Richard Byrd (U.S.A.)

In 1929 Byrd set up an expedition base so he and his men could spend the winter in Antarctica. He called the base "Little America." On November 28 Byrd and his crew made the first flight across the South Pole. They had to throw out all the emergency rations to gain enough altitude to make it over the high mountains.

Byrd returned to Antarctica many times, making weather observations and charting the land. He commanded Operation Highjump in 1946 in which airplanes were used to take photos to map vast areas of land. In 1956 he commanded Operation Deep Freeze, a series of expeditions that established five coastal research stations and three inland stations, including one at the South Pole.

9

Borge Ousland (Norway)

Although most of the exploration of Antarctica today occurs at research stations operated by scientists and technicians, there are still individuals seeking to conquer the icy continent alone. Borge Ousland is one such person. In 1996 he began a trek to the South Pole. After traveling 1675 miles in 64 days, Ousland became the first person to cross Antarctica alone.

10

Name

A Time Line of Exploration

Write the name of each explorer in the correct box to complete the time line.
Add other dates, explorers, and events as you learn more about the exploration of Antarctica.

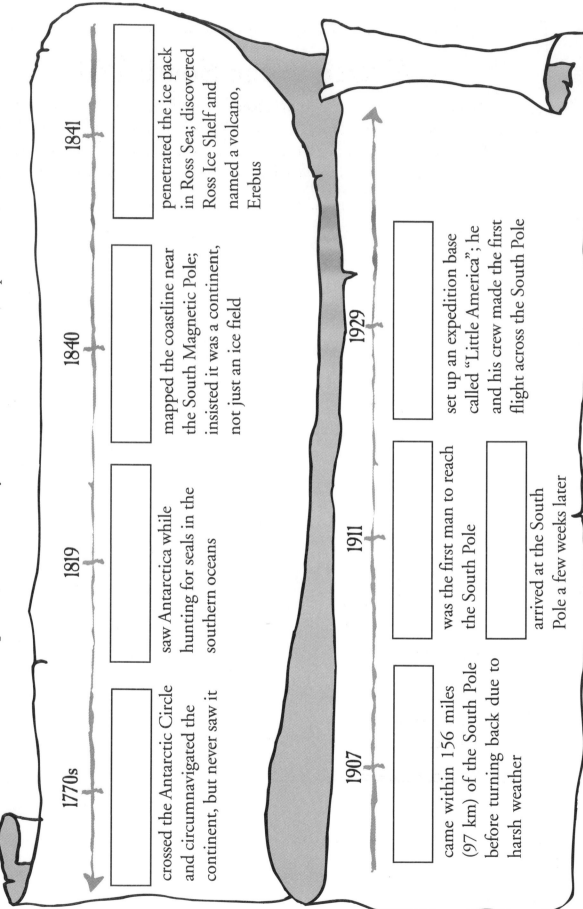

1841
penetrated the ice pack in Ross Sea; discovered Ross Ice Shelf and named a volcano, Erebus

1840
mapped the coastline near the South Magnetic Pole; insisted it was a continent, not just an ice field

1819
saw Antarctica while hunting for seals in the southern oceans

1770s
crossed the Antarctic Circle and circumnavigated the continent, but never saw it

1929
set up an expedition base called "Little America"; he and his crew made the first flight across the South Pole

1911
was the first man to reach the South Pole

arrived at the South Pole a few weeks later

1907
came within 156 miles (97 km) of the South Pole before turning back due to harsh weather

A Race to the South Pole

In 1911 Captain Robert Falcon Scott and Roald Amundsen set off on separate expeditions attempting to reach the South Pole. Both men were determined to be the first to reach that goal. Use class resources to learn more about these two men and how they planned and conducted their expeditions. Record what you learn on the comparison chart.

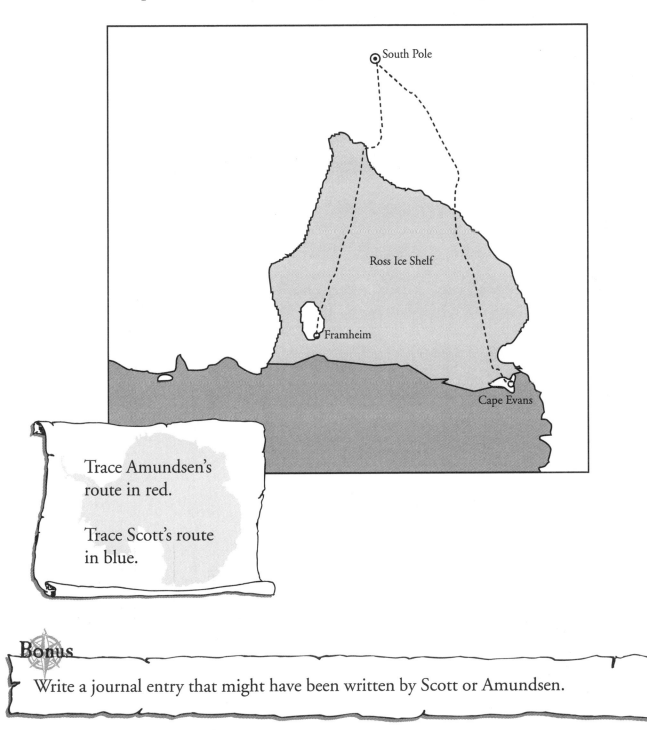

Trace Amundsen's route in red.

Trace Scott's route in blue.

Bonus

Write a journal entry that might have been written by Scott or Amundsen.

Exploration Comparison Chart

	🇬🇧 Scott	🇳🇴 Amundsen
Preparation		
Key events on journey		
Date arrived at the South Pole		
Return journey		

The People

While there is no permanent population living in Antarctica, there are a few thousand people working at special science research stations. The scientists, technicians, and support personnel at these stations must deal with extreme weather conditions most of the time. (There are many excellent sites on the World Wide Web for students learning about research stations in Antarctica.)

Science Research Stations

Reproduce pages 49–51 for each student. Read and discuss the information together. Ask students to look at the locations of the stations on the map. Ask, "Why are so many of the stations located along the coasts of Antarctica?"

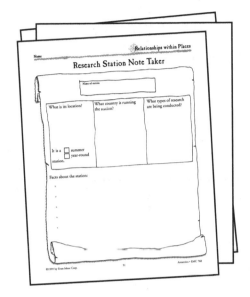

Divide students into small groups. Assign McMurdo Station or Amundsen-Scott Station to each group. Students are to do the following:

- use class resources, including the World Wide Web, to learn about the station
- record information on their note takers (page 51)
- present what they discovered to the rest of the class

Research Station Locations

Using a Compass Rose

Reproduce pages 50 and 52 for each student. Use the compass rose on the unit map to review how to determine location using cardinal directions. Then have students complete the activity independently.

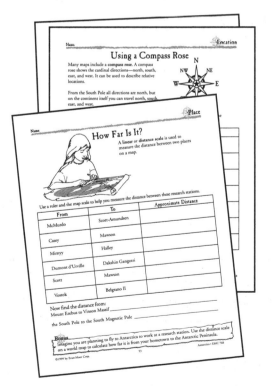

How Far Is It?

Reproduce pages 50 and 53 for each student. Use the unit map to review how to use a map scale to figure distances. Then have students use a ruler and the map scale to determine the distance between various research stations on Antarctica.

Life at a Science Research Station

Reproduce the information on pages 54–57 for each student. Read and discuss the material together. As you read, answer the questions on page 56. Then have students complete page 57, identifying the various types of scientists working at the stations.

Who Owns Antarctica?

Reproduce pages 58 and 59. Read and discuss the information together. Have students use class resources to complete the diagram showing who has claimed portions of Antarctica.

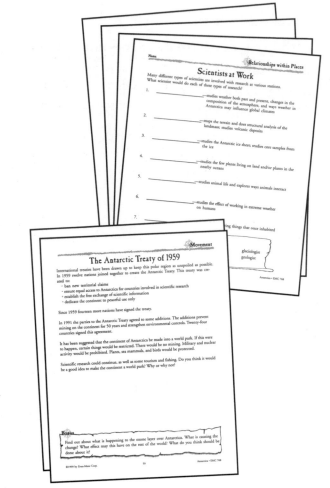

Science Research Stations

The scientists and technicians at research stations are the major explorers of Antarctica today. The stations range in size and number of people. McMurdo is the largest station in Antarctica. It is like a small town containing several hundred people. Amundsen-Scott Station at the South Pole is a small station. It is also the highest of the research stations at 9300 feet (2835 m) altitude.

Many countries maintain research stations. Stations work independently, with scientists conducting research in many areas. Information is often shared among the various research stations.

The location and design of a research station must take into consideration the harsh weather conditions under which people will be working and living. Much planning and care goes into determining what materials will be needed by the station crew—clothing, food and fuel, means of communication and transportation, and medical emergencies must all be considered. Station personnel must be competent, healthy, and able to withstand the isolation and close quarters of smaller stations.

In addition to the scientists and technicians involved in research, many support people are needed, especially at the larger stations. Buildings need to be constructed, food needs to be prepared, injuries need to be tended, etc. All of these support positions are important for the smooth operation of a station.

Research Station

While most stations do research only during the Antarctic summer months, some research teams stay throughout the year.

Imagine you are going to a research station. What job would you like to do?

Research Stations

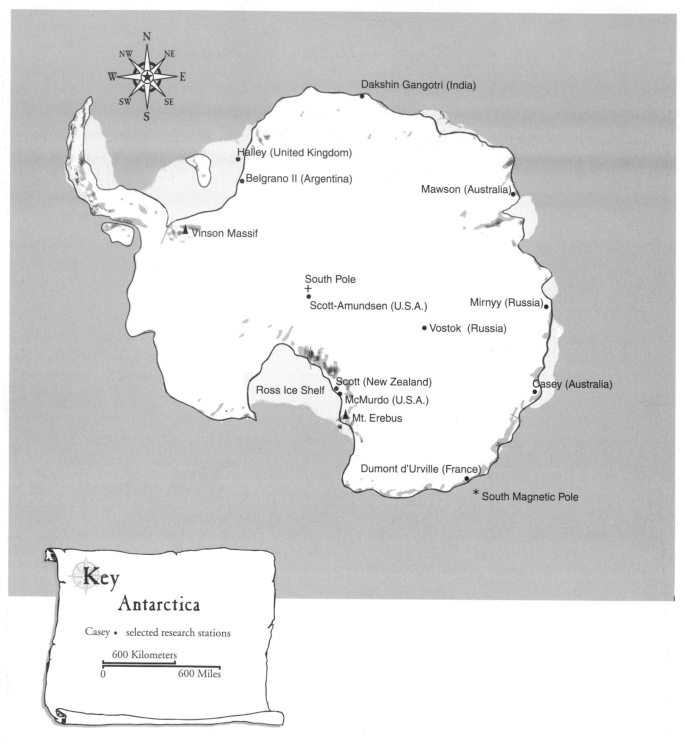

Research Station Note Taker

Name of station

What is its location?	What country is running the station?	What types of research are being conducted?
It is a ☐ summer ☐ year-round station.		

Facts about the station:

- •
- •
- •
- •
- •

Using a Compass Rose

Many maps include a **compass rose**. A compass rose shows the cardinal directions—north, south, east, and west. It can be used to describe relative locations.

From the South Pole all directions are north, but on the continent itself you can travel north, south, east, and west.

Use the compass rose on your map to find the direction you would travel between the places listed below.

From	To	Direction
South Magnetic Pole	Vinson Massif	
Ross Ice Shelf	South Pole	
Scott Research Station	Mt. Erebus	
Casey Research Station	Scott Research Station	
Belgrano II Research Station	Casey Research Station	
Halley Research Station	Vostok Research Station	
Vinson Massif	Mt. Erebus	

How Far Is It?

A **linear** or **distance scale** is used to measure the distance between two places on a map.

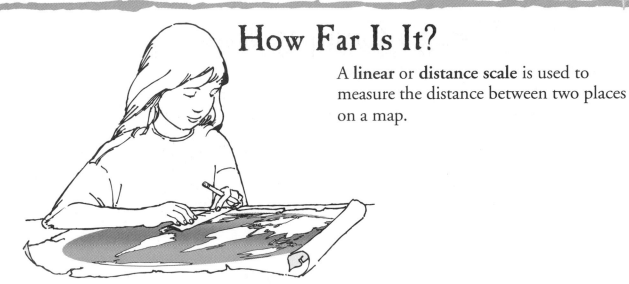

Use a ruler and the map scale to help you measure the distance between these research stations.

From	To	Approximate Distance
McMurdo	Scott-Amundsen	
Casey	Mawson	
Mirnyy	Halley	
Dumont d'Urville	Dakshin Gangotri	
Scott	Mawson	
Vostok	Belgrano II	

Now find the distance from:
• Mount Erebus to Vinson Massif _____

• the South Pole to the South Magnetic Pole _____

Bonus

Imagine you are planning to fly to Antarctica to work at a research station. Use the distance scale on a world map to calculate how far it is from your hometown to the Antarctic Peninsula.

Life at a Research Station

Life for people working at a research station today is very different from the hardships faced by camps established by the early explorers and researchers.

Food

People at the research stations eat many of the same foods they would eat at home. Careful thought has to go into determining how much food and what types of food are necessary. This is especially important for research stations that remain active throughout the year. Due to the harsh winter weather, all the supplies needed for a year must be delivered during the summer months. Meat and other perishable foods are stored in freezers. Large research stations have a cooking staff responsible for preparing three meals a day for everyone working at the station.

Clothing

What a person wears depends on several factors—the temperature, the wind level, and whether the work is indoors or outside. When dressing in Antarctica, it is important to remember the word "layers." By wearing several layers of clothing, clothing can be removed or added as needed.

People working indoors wear the same types of clothing they would wear anywhere. People in the field may wear four or five layers of clothing. The outer layer is almost always something waterproof. Outside in the winter when the temperature falls many degrees below zero and the wind is blowing, a worker might wear the following:
- long underwear, pants and a sweater, and insulated outer pants
- thick wool socks and insulated boots
- down-filled parka
- wool glove liners and thick leather mittens
- warm hat with earflaps and a balaclava
- a warm scarf or band around your neck
- goggles
- chemical hand warmers in gloves and boots

How do you dress to go outdoors in winter where you live?

Antarctic Research Station

Buildings

Buildings in Antarctica must be designed to withstand blowing and drifting snow and high winds. Newer buildings are designed to allow wind to blow around or underneath them. Entrances are placed out of the direct path of the wind. This helps keep snow from blowing into the building and saves heat and energy. Walls have thick insulation. Water and plumbing pipes are wrapped with insulation to prevent freezing.

There are toilets in dormitories and some other buildings. Smaller stations and some field camps have "outhouses." Sewer lines and water lines are above ground so the leaks and freezing problems can be found. Everyone in Antarctica must be careful not to waste water. Some research stations have desalination plants to make fresh water from seawater; other stations melt ice for fresh water.

Solar panels, wind-turbine generators, and fueled motor generators all contribute to the fuel supply needed to heat buildings and run equipment used by the people living and working in the buildings.

Transportation and Communication

Ships, airplanes, and helicopters are used to transport people and supplies in Antarctica. Ships called icebreakers are used to break through ocean ice. Land vehicles such as tractors and snowcats are used around research stations. Roads between buildings and helicopter pads have been built. Some research stations have runways for planes.

Research stations communicate within Antarctica and with the outside world using telephones, satellites, and high-frequency radios. When groups go out into the field, they carry radios, extra batteries, and solar panels for recharging the batteries. The groups are to call in once a day so the home base can keep track of them. Anyone going to a very remote area also wears a small beacon, which can send emergency messages to satellites. Computers and the World Wide Web are also used to keep in contact with the rest of the world.

How is life at a research station the same as life in your hometown?
How is life at a research station different from life in your hometown?

Bonus

Imagine you are being sent to explore an area in the interior of the continent. You will be gone several days. Decide how you will travel and what you will need to take with you. Make a list of supplies. Draw yourself dressed for this adventure.

Pollution

From the earliest days of exploration, trash, human waste, and other pollution have been left behind. Today, empty fuel drums and vehicles of all kinds have been abandoned. Human waste and other garbage have been dumped. Abandoned research stations have been left rather than torn down.

In recent years, some stations have taken steps to reduce the buildup of garbage and other pollution. This has not been consistent among the many stations, especially at field camps where everything must be carried back to a base camp.

Environmental groups are keeping a close watch on what is happening to the continent. They are especially concerned about what could happen in the near future.

Think about these questions:
- Will the increased number of people working in and visiting Antarctica affect the animal life?
- Will the emerging krill-harvesting industry create an imbalance in the ecosystem?
- Will the rate of depletion of the world's crude-oil reserves cause countries to begin looking at the possibility of trying to reach the oil under the thick ice cap?
- Some people think the continent should be permanently protected from development. What do you think?

Show what Antarctica will look like if pollution is not controlled.

Scientists at Work

Many different types of scientists are involved with research at various stations. What scientist would do each of these types of research?

1. _____ —studies weather both past and present, changes in the composition of the atmosphere, and ways weather in Antarctica may influence global climates

2. _____ —maps the terrain and does structural analysis of the landmass; studies volcanic deposits

3. _____ —studies the Antarctic ice sheet; studies core samples from the ice

4. _____ —studies the few plants living on land and/or plants in the nearby oceans

5. _____ —studies animal life and explores ways animals interact

6. _____ —studies the effect of working in extreme weather on humans

7. _____ —studies fossils of living things that once inhabited the Antarctic

Word Box

	botanist	glaciologist
biologist	meteorologist	geologist
medical researcher	paleontologist	

Who Owns Antarctica?

Under the ice of Antarctica, there is land. As explorers worked their way toward the South Pole, they made claims for their countries. A map of Antarctica showing these claims looks like a pie cut into pieces, with the lines radiating out from the geographical pole in the center.

This map shows the area claimed by Australia. Use class resources to locate and label other countries' claims.

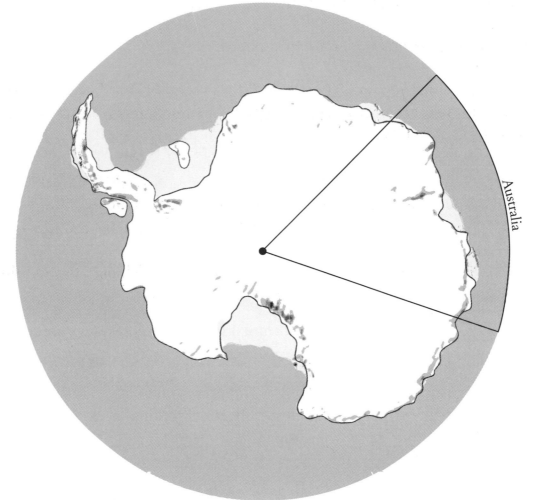

Australia

Use the diagram to answer these questions:

1. Which country has claimed the largest portion of the continent? _____

2. Which country has claimed the smallest portion of the continent? _____

3. How many countries have made claims to part of Antarctica? _____

4. Has your country claimed part of Antarctica? If yes, color in that portion.

The Antarctic Treaty of 1959

International treaties have been drawn up to keep this polar region as unspoiled as possible. In 1959 twelve nations joined together to create the Antarctic Treaty. This treaty was created to:

- ban new territorial claims
- ensure equal access to Antarctica for countries involved in scientific research
- establish the free exchange of scientific information
- dedicate the continent to peaceful use only

Since 1959 fourteen more nations have signed the treaty.

In 1991 the parties to the Antarctic Treaty agreed to some additions. The additions prevent mining on the continent for 50 years and strengthen environmental controls. Twenty-four countries signed this agreement.

It has been suggested that the continent of Antarctica be made into a world park. If this were to happen, certain things would be restricted. There would be no mining. Military and nuclear activity would be prohibited. Plants, sea mammals, and birds would be protected.

Scientific research could continue, as well as some tourism and fishing. Do you think it would be a good idea to make the continent a world park? Why or why not?

Bonus

Find out about what is happening to the ozone layer over Antarctica. What is causing the change? What effect may this have on the rest of the world? What do you think should be done about it?

The Arctic

Both ends of the Earth are remote with harsh climates, but they are different in major ways. The physical geography is different—Antarctica is land surrounded by water; the Arctic is water surrounded by land. The life, plants, animals, and the humans are also different.

Your students may not understand these differences, assuming that because they are icy regions they are alike in other ways. The activities in this section help students identify the differences and similarities between the two areas.

The Arctic and Antarctica

Reproduce pages 61 and 62 for each student. First ask students to think of ways the Arctic (North Pole) and Antarctica (South Pole) are alike and different. Record these on a sheet of chart paper. Then read and discuss both pages together. Make additions and corrections to the chart.

Arctic Plants and Animals

Share books such as *Polar Wildlife* to learn about Arctic plants and animals. Have students compile a list of Arctic plants and animals as they explore resources in the geography center.

People of the Arctic

Reproduce page 63 for each student. Read and discuss the information together. Provide books such as *Eskimo Boy—Life in an Inupiaq Eskimo Village, Arctic Hunter,* and *Far North* for students to use as they explore people living in the Arctic. Have students share what they learn with the rest of the class.

Comparing the Poles

Reproduce page 64 for each student. Students are to use what they have learned to compare and contrast the Arctic and Antarctica.

The Arctic and Antarctica

Antarctica	The Arctic
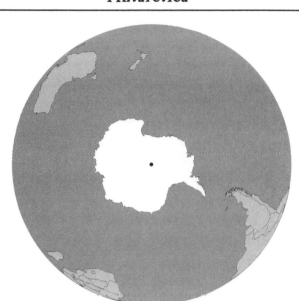	
Antarctica is a continent surrounded by water. It is almost twice the size of the United States and is the southernmost place on Earth. It contains 90% of the world's ice.	When you look at a map of the Arctic, you are not looking at land. What you see is ice. Most of the Arctic is a frozen ocean of ice surrounded by land. The northern edges of Alaska, Canada, Greenland, Norway, Sweden, Finland, and Russia border the Arctic.
Antarctica is the coldest place on Earth. It is also very windy and very dry. Between its climate and its poor soil, Antarctica has few plants and animals living on the land. However, the sea around Antarctica is filled with life.	It is cold all year long in the Arctic. During the dark months the temperatures are extremely cold. As the days grow longer, it warms up enough to allow a short spring and summer to occur. Plants bloom and animals roam about. There are many land animals at the Arctic.
Antarctica has six months of darkness, followed by six months of light.	At the North Pole the periods of light and darkness are the opposite of Antarctica. When Antarctica has six months of light, the Arctic has six months of darkness. When it is dark in Antarctica, it is light in the Arctic.
Because it is located on top of a great continental ice sheet, the South Pole is over 9000 feet (about 2800 m) above sea level.	

Name

·Place

Arctic Plants and Animals

Plants

The land around the Arctic Ocean is called the tundra. Even in the summer it is cold and windy in the Arctic. This makes it hard for plants to grow. However, during the long summer days, the ice on the surface of the tundra melts. This provides a chance for plants to grow.

Mosses, grasses, and lichen are the most common plants growing in the warmer weather and increased sunlight. There are many kinds of flowering plants. But there are no big bushes or trees.

The plants provide food for many of the animals living in the Arctic. Animals that don't eat the plants eat other animals that do.

Arctic Poppy

Snowy Owl

Animals

The weather is somewhat less harsh in the Arctic than in Antarctica. You will find a wider number of animals living on land and in the water there, especially during the warmer spring and summer months. Some live on the tundra surrounding the Arctic Ocean, some live on the pack ice, and others live in the sea. Many birds migrate to the Arctic during the summer season.

The animals have special body adaptations (thick fur, layers of fat, number and arrangement of feathers) to help protect them from the cold. Some animals fatten up during the warm months, then hibernate when the cold winter begins. Other animals migrate to warmer areas when it becomes too cold.

Use class resources to find out about plants and animals living in the Arctic. On the back of this page, make a list of plants and animals that you read about. Circle any plants or animals on your list that also live in Antarctica.

People of the Arctic

There have been people living in the Arctic for thousands of years. These people have adapted to the cold climate and long, dark winters. Most of these people settled along the coasts where they could fish and hunt animals such as seals and whales.

The Saami have lived above the Arctic Circle in the far northern parts of Scandinavia for hundreds of years. They are a nomadic people traveling from place to place with their herds of reindeer. They move their herds across the plateaus and up into the Arctic Mountains in the summer, then back down to the plateaus in the winter. They live in tents and use reindeer for clothing, food, and transportation. This way of life is changing rapidly as the Saami have more contact with modern civilizations. More of the Saami have settled in towns. Many of them herd their reindeer with snowmobiles and purchase clothing, food, and other goods from stores. Others now live in towns and cities where they work at jobs such as carpenters, clerks, doctors, and teachers.

Also living in the Arctic are the Inuit. The word Inuit means "human being." They share the ability to survive in an extremely harsh land, using the natural materials and available animals for their homes, clothing, and food. As with the Saami, the traditional ways have changed with the arrival of modern ways of life. Arctic peoples must now live in two worlds. There is more contact between traditional villages and modern towns and cities. Hunters use modern weapons, and snowmobiles are replacing sled dogs. Many Inuit have moved to cities in Alaska and Canada.

There are many native cultures in the Arctic, each having its own history, traditions, and language.

Use class resources to learn more about the Saami or Inuit. Share what you learn on another page.

Past

Present

Compare the Poles

Read each sentence. Check boxes to show whether the statement is true about the Arctic, Antarctica, or both.

	Arctic	Antarctica	Both
The location of the pole is on land.			
The location of the pole is in the ocean.			
The temperature is below freezing much of the year.			
There are many groups of native peoples living here.			
There is no native population.			
Penguins live here.			
This area is a continent.			
Icebergs can be found here.			
The land touches the Indian Ocean.			
This polar region is in the southern hemisphere.			
Walruses live here.			
There is land under the ice.			
The coldest place on Earth is found here.			
Admiral Richard Byrd explored here.			
This polar region is in the northern hemisphere.			

Celebrate Learning

Choose one or all of the following activities to celebrate the culmination of your unit on Antarctica. Use the activities to help assess student learning.

Have a Portfolio Party

Invite parents and other interested people to a "portfolio party" where students will share their completed portfolios, as well as other projects about Antarctica.

Write a Book

A student can make a book about Antarctica. It might be one of the following:
- a nonfiction story about the exploration of Antarctica
- a dictionary of words pertaining to Antarctica
- a pop-up book of the life cycle of a penguin
- a riddle book about locations, landforms, or animals

Conduct an Interview

A student can interview someone who has been to Antarctica or is an expert on the continent. The interview could be in person, written about, or videotaped to share with the class.

Create a Skit

One or more students can write and present a skit about one of the early expeditions to Antarctica or a day in the life of a scientist at one of the research stations.

Paint a Mural

One or more students can paint a mural showing some aspect of life in Antarctica (penguin rookery, research station, interesting land formation). A chart of facts about the region should accompany the mural.

Build a Diorama

One or more students can build a diorama modeling an Antarctic landform, animal habitat, explorer, or research station.

Note: Reproduce this form for each student. Use it throughout the unit to record basic information. (See page 6.)

Name ______________________________ Summary of Facts

Antarctica

Relative location ______________________

Land area ______________________

Highest point ______________________

Lowest point ______________________

Coldest temperature ______________________

Major life forms ______________________

____

Description of climate ______________________

____

____

Interesting facts about the continent:

- ______________________
- ______________________
- ______________________
- ______________________
- ______________________

Interesting facts about the animals:

- ______________________
- ______________________
- ______________________
- ______________________
- ______________________

Name _____

What's Inside This Portfolio?

Date	What It Is	Why I Put It In

Name

My Bibliography

Date	Title	Author/Publisher	Kind of Resource

Search

Name a type of flightless bird found in Antarctica.

1

Search

What time of year does Antarctica have its shortest days and longest nights?

2

Search

What is the highest point on Antarctica? How high is it?

3

Search

Why is the continent of Antarctica considered a desert?

4

Search

Name the longest mountain range in Antarctica.

5

Search

What is the name of the last volcano to erupt in Antarctica?

6

Search

What is Antarctica's coldest recorded temperature?

7

Search

What is another name for the southern lights?

8

Search

How long is the Transantarctic Mountain Range?

9

Search

What types of trees grow in Antarctica?

10

Search

Why is Antarctica sometimes called "the home of the wind"?

11

Search

Who led the first group of explorers to reach the South Pole?

12

Search

Why can't you travel south from the South Pole?

13

Search

Who owns Antarctica?

14

Search

What country established McMurdo Research Station?

15

Search

Name the two continents that are smaller in land area than Antarctica.

16

Search

What percentage of Antarctica is covered in ice and snow?

17

Search

What is the difference between a glacier and an iceberg?

18

Search

What percentage of the world's fresh water supply is frozen in Antarctica's ice cap?

19

Search

Which group of whales eats krill?

20

Search

What is the most feared predator in Antarctica?

21

Search

Which type of whale hunts in groups to catch its prey?

22

Search

What type of penguin is this? How can you tell?

23

Search

Which continent is closest to Antarctica?

24

Search

Name the largest of Antarctica's ice shelves.

25

Search

What is Captain James Cook's connection with Antarctica?

26

Search

Who is the second person recorded to reach the South Pole?

27

Name

Antarctica

Word Box

iceberg
moss
Mt. Erebus
penguin
rookeries
sea
sea ice

seal
skua
snow
southern lights
South Pole
stations
Vinson Massif

Adélie
Antarctica
glacier
ice

Across

2. a type of penguin
4. a large body of salt water
6. bright, glowing lights moving in the night sky in the southern polar areas
7. a type of small, flowerless plant growing in parts of Antarctica
10. a mass of floating ice that has broken off a glacier
11. a mammal living in the sea along the coast of Antarctica
14. places where communities of penguins lay their eggs and raise their young
15. the highest point on Antarctica

Down

1. the most southern pole of Earth
2. the fifth largest continent
3. frozen water
5. a large mass of ice formed from compacted snow
6. lacy flakes of frozen water
8. a type of large sea gull that preys on penguin eggs and chicks
9. a flightless bird found in Antarctica and nearby areas
11. ice formed by the freezing of sea water
12. Antarctica's active volcano
13. scientists work at research _____

Antarctica

```
C C A N T A R C T I C A I S N O W R
S O U T H M A G N E T I C P O L E O
M N L X S E A M U N D S E N W X D O
O T O D K R I L L T O C B E F G D K
S I N W U Y P O L A R O E P R L E E
S N C O A I S O U T H T R S E A L R
P E O E W C W H A L E T G N E C L Y
E N O P R E D A T O R S N O Z I S R
N T K R E S E A R C H U P W E E E O
G S L I C H E N E M P E R O R R A S
U N Q U E E N M A U D L A N D A Z S
I O C E A L T E M P E R A T U R E S
N W O N S F L I G H T L E S S E R E
V I N S O N M A S S I F S N O W O A
X A N T A R C T I C C I R C L E X A
A U R O R A A U S T R A L I S T O O
```

Find these words:

Amery Ice Shelf	glacier	Ross Sea
Amundsen	ice	Scott
Antarctica	iceberg	seal
Antarctic Circle	krill	skua
Aurora Australis	lichen	snow
cold	moss	south
continent	penguin	South Magnetic Pole
Cook	predator	temperature
emperor	polar	Vinson Massif
flightless	Queen Maud Land	Weddell Sea
freeze	research	whale
	rookery	zero

Antarctica • EMC 768

Glossary

absolute location (exact location)–the location of a point that can be expressed exactly, for example, the intersection of a line of longitude and latitude.

algae–small plants, sometimes only one cell, that live in damp places and can make their own food; no true stem, roots, or leaves.

Antarctic Circle–an imaginary line circling the globe at 66.5°S latitude.

Arctic Circle–an imaginary line circling the globe at 66.5°N latitude.

Aurora Australis–also called the southern lights; moving streams or curtains of light in the sky caused by the interaction of charged particles from the sun with the Earth's atmosphere.

balaclava–a knitted hat that covers the face as well as the head.

bay–a body of water partly enclosed by land.

blizzard–a violent windstorm with driving snow and intense cold; a heavy snowstorm.

climate–the type of weather a region has over a long period of time.

compass rose–the drawing on a map that shows the cardinal directions.

continent–one of the main landmasses on Earth (usually counted as seven—Antarctica, Australia, Africa, North America, South America, Asia, and Europe).

crevasse–a deep cleft in the ice of a glacier.

floe–a large mass of floating ice broken from a glacier, an ice shelf, or sea ice.

glacier–a large mass of ice that moves slowly down the side of a mountain or along a valley.

gulf–a portion of an ocean or sea partly enclosed by land.

hemisphere–half of a sphere; one of the halves into which the Earth is divided—western hemisphere, eastern hemisphere, southern hemisphere, or northern hemisphere.

iceberg–a large mass of ice that has broken off a glacier and is floating in the sea.

ice cap–a sheet of ice and snow that permanently covers an area.

isthmus–a narrow strip of land bordered on both sides by water.

krill–small shrimplike animals found in the ocean which are the primary food source for many Antarctic animals.

landform–the shape, form, or nature of a physical feature on Earth's surface (mountain, plateau, hill, glacier, etc.).

latitude–the position of a point on Earth's surface measured in degrees, north or south from the equator.

lichen–a flowerless plant that grows on rocks and other surfaces; composed of a fungus and an alga in a symbiotic relationship.

longitude–the distance east or west of Greenwich meridian (0° longitude) measured in degrees.

meridian–an imaginary circle running north/south, passing through the poles and any point on the Earth's surface.

moss–small, soft green plants growing in clumps on moist ground, rocks, etc.

North Pole–the northernmost point on Earth; the northern end of the Earth's axis.

peninsula–an area of water almost completely surrounded by water.

plankton–microscopic plants and animals living near the surface of a body of water.

plateau–an area of land with a relatively level surface considerably raised above adjoining land on at least one side.

Prime meridian (Greenwich meridian)–the longitude line at 0° from which other lines of longitude are measured.

relative location–the location of a point on the Earth's surface in relation to other points.

resource–substances or materials that people value and use; a means of meeting a need for food, shelter, warmth, transportation, etc.

rookery–the colony, or breeding grounds, of seals, seabirds, and many other animals.

scale–indication of the ratio between a given distance on the map to the corresponding distance on the Earth's surface.

sea ice–ice that forms when seawater freezes, as compared to the frozen freshwater of glaciers and icebergs.

South Pole–the southernmost point on Earth; the southern end of the Earth's axis.

strait–a narrow passage of water connecting two large bodies of water.

symbol–something that represents a real thing.

tundra–a cold, barren area where much of the soil is frozen and vegetation consists only of small plants.

Answer Key

Page 16
1. Point A–0 feet (sea level)
   Point B–5 thousand feet
   Point C–⁻5 thousand feet or 5 thousand feet below sea level
   Point D–8 thousand feet
   Point E–⁻5 thousand feet or 5 thousand feet below sea level
   Point F–5 thousand feet
2. about 10 thousand feet

Page 18
1. Ross Sea
2. Queen Maud Land
3. Polar Plateau
4. Weddell Sea
5. Vinson Massif
6. Wilkes Land
7. Amundsen Sea
8. Shackelton Ice Shelf
9. Filchner Ice Shelf
10. Amery Ice Shelf

Page 22
1. Glaciers are formed from snow that fell thousands of years ago. The snow didn't melt. It packed down into a solid sheet of ice.
2. The heavy weight of the glacier causes it to move down sloping land.
3. A glacier is an ice mass on land. An iceberg is an ice mass that has broken off into the sea.
4. Between 6/7ths and 9/10ths of an iceberg is underwater.
5. The movement of wind and water blowing against the iceberg melts it into strange shapes.
6. Small bubbles of air in ice make it look white. When the heavy weight of ice compresses it, the air is squeezed out and the ice looks blue.

Page 24
1. The peninsula is long and thin, reaching out into the Atlantic Ocean toward South America.
2. It is approximately 600 miles (966 km) from the tip of South America.
3. It is the northernmost part of Antarctica. Prevailing winds and currents make this area warmer than the rest of the continent.
4. Chinstrap, Adélie, and Southern Gentoo
5. algae, moss, lichen, and two kinds of flowering plants (a grass and a flower); they get the water they need during the summer months, when the 24-hour days of sunshine melt the ice

Page 28
1. lichen–a flowerless plant that grows on rocks or other surfaces; composed of a fungus and an alga
   algae–small plants with no roots, stems, or leaves that grow in damp places
   moss–small, soft green plants growing in clumps on moist rocks and ground
2. It is too cold and the soil, where it exists, is too poor in nutrients.
3. The water is warmer than the land and it is richer in nutrients.

Page 31

	Emperor	Adélie	Gentoo	Chinstrap
Height	about 45" (115 cm)	about 27.5" (70 cm)	about 29.5" (75 cm)	about 27" (69 cm)
Weight	about 66 lb (30 kg)	about 11 lb (5 kg)	about 13 lb (6 kg)	about 10 lb (4.5 kg)
Markings	black back, feet, head, & wings; white chest; yellow on sides of neck	black head, back, & wings; white chest; white circle around eyes; orange feet	black head, back, & wings; white chest & marking over head; orange & black beak; orange feet	black back, wings, beak, & top of head; white on sides of head; black line under chin
Nesting habits	doesn't build a nest; lays one egg	nest of pebbles; lays 2 eggs	nest of pebbles; lays 2 eggs	nest of pebbles; lays 2 eggs
Egg care	male carries eggs on feet & covers it with warm stomach pouch	parents take turns sitting on eggs	parents take turns sitting on eggs	parents take turns sitting on eggs
Chick care	parents take turns going to sea for fish to feed chick; other parent keeps chick safe & warm	parents take turns going to sea for krill to feed chicks; other parent keeps chicks safe & warm	parents take turns going to sea for krill & fish to feed chicks; other parent keeps chicks safe & warm	parents take turns going to sea for krill to feed chicks; other parent keeps chicks safe & warm

Pages 35 and 36
Answers will vary.

Page 46

	Scott	Amundsen
Preparation	Brought a kind of motorized sled, Siberian ponies, dogs, & several tons of supplies. Men went to work immediately and continued to work long days as they set up camp and supply depots. Marked depots with a flag or a can on a stick.	Brought huskies, a prefabricated hut, & provisions for 2 years. Men rested regularly as they set up camp and supply depots. Marked depots with many flags.
Key events on journey	Set out Oct. 24 to cross Ross Ice Shelf. Used sleds for a short time before they broke down. Last of ponies dead by December. Blizzards began in December. Sent dogs back to camp. Men had to use their own strength from then on. Climbed Beardmore Glacier and then crossed the Antarctic Plateau. Scott and four men went on to South Pole. After weeks of struggle, reached South Pole to discover Amundsen had already been there.	Set out on Oct. 20. Men rode on sleds pulled by dogs. Left a supply depot several places along the way. Crossed Axel Heiberg Glacier. Then started across the Antarctic Plateau. Amundsen and four men set off for the South Pole. They remained at the pole for three days, then, with two sleds in 38 days, returned home.
Date arrived at the South Pole	January 17, 1912	December 14, 1911
Return journey	Scott and the four men that went with him to the South Pole all died on the return trip.	Amundsen and his men reached home base safely.

Page 69

1. a penguin
2. the winter months, April through September
3. Vinson Massif–16,864 feet (5140 m)
4. The average precipitation (in the form of snow) is only 4" (10 cm) per year.
5. Transantarctic Mountains
6. Mt. Erebus
7. ⁻129° F (⁻89.4° C)
8. Aurora Australis
9. It is 2175 miles (3500 km) long, running from the Ross Sea to the Weddell Sea.

Page 70

10. No trees grow in Antarctica.
11. The frequently blowing wind can reach up to 200 miles (322 km) per hour.
12. Norway's Roald Amundsen–Dec. 14, 1911
13. It is as far south as you can go in any direction.
14. Several countries have made claims on parts of Antarctica, but currently no one owns the continent.
15. the United States
16. Australia and Europe
17. over 90%
18. A glacier is on land; an iceberg is in the ocean.

Page 71

19. 70%
20. the baleen whales
21. the leopard seal
22. the killer whale (orca)
23. a chinstrap penguin; has a line under its beak that looks like the strap of a cap
24. South America
25. the Ross Ice Shelf; contains 30% of Antarctica's ice
26. He circumnavigated the continent in the 1770s.
27. Captain Robert Falcon Scott

Page 72

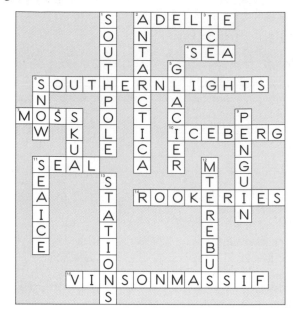

Page 74

Bibliography

Books about Antarctica

Adventure at the Top/Bottom of the World by Shelley Gill; Paws IV Publishing, 1996.

Antarctic Journal by James Hasick; A Keystone Book, 1993.

Antarctica by John Baines; Raintree Steck-Vaughn Publishers, 1998.

Antarctica: Beyond the Southern Ocean by Colin Monteath; Barrons Educational Series, Inc., 1997.

Antarctica: The Last Continent by Kim Heacox; National Geographic Society, 1998.

Antarctica: The Last Unspoiled Continent by Laurence Pringle; Simon and Schuster Books for Young Readers, 1992.

Our Endangered Planet—Antarctica by Suzanne Winckler and Mary M. Rodgers; Lerner Publications Company, 1992.

Penguin: A Season in the Life of the Adélie Penguin by Lloyd Spencer Davis; Harcourt Brace Jovanovich, 1994.

Penguins by Roger T. Peterson; Houghton Mifflin Company, 1998.

Polar Wildlife; Usborne Publishing Ltd., 1992.

Science on the Ice: An Antarctic Journal (Discovery!) by Rebecca L. Johnson; Lerner Publications Company, 1995.

Summer Ice: Life Along the Antarctic Peninsula by Bruce McMillan; Houghton Mifflin Company, 1995.

The Arctic and Antarctica, Roof and Floor of the World by Alice Gilbreath; Dillon Press, Inc., 1988.

The Cruelest Place on Earth: Stories from Antarctica by John Nicholson; Allen & Unwin Pty Ltd., 1994.

Trapped by the Ice!: Shackleton's Amazing Antarctic Adventure by Michael McCurdy; Walker Publishing Company, Inc., 1997.

Books about the Arctic

Arctic Hunter by Diane Hoyt-Goldsmith; Holiday House, 1992.

Eskimo Boy—Life in an Inupiaq Eskimo Village by Russ Kendall; Scholastic Inc., 1992.

Far North (Vanishing Cultures Series) by Jan Reynolds; Harcourt Brace Jovanovich, 1992.

In Two Worlds: A Yup'ik Eskimo Family by Aylette Jenness and Alice Rivers; Houghton Mifflin Company, 1989.

General Reference Books

(Maps and atlases published before 1997 may not have the latest changes in country names and borders, but they will still contain much valuable material.)

Atlas of Continents; Rand McNally & Company, 1996.

National Geographic Concise Atlas of the World; National Geographic Society, 1997.

National Geographic Picture Atlas of Our World; National Geographic Society, 1994.

The New Puffin Children's World Atlas by Jacqueline Tivers and Michael Day; Puffin Books, 1995.

The Reader's Digest Children's Atlas of the World; Consulting Editor: Colin Sale; Joshua Morris Publishing, Inc., 1998.

The World Almanac and Book of Facts 1998; Editorial Director: Robert Famighetti; K-III Reference Corporation, 1997.

Technology

Videos

Antarctica produced by National Geographic Society, 1991.

Antarctic Adventure produced by Fenton McHugh; Bennet Marine Video, 1989.

Antarctic Wildlife Adventure produced by National Geographic Society, 1991.

CD-ROM and Disks

Encarta® Encyclopedia; ©Microsoft Corporation (CD-ROM).

MacGlobe & PC Globe; Broderbund (disk).

Where in the World Is Carmen Sandiego?; Broderbund (CD-ROM and disk).

World Fact Book; Bureau of Electronic Publishing Inc. (CD-ROM).

Zip Zap Map; National Geographic (laser disc and disk).

Websites

For sites on the World Wide Web that supplement the material in this resource book, go to http://www.evan-moor.com.